IMAGES
of America

# WEST HOLLYWOOD

West Hollywood can be seen from the roof of city hall, along with Santa Monica Boulevard and the West Hollywood Hills. The high rise hotels and buildings took root in the development of the later part of the 20th century, making West Hollywood one of the newest looking new cities in America. With 37,000 residents in just under two square miles, it is also one of the more densely packed neighborhoods in the country. The recent (finished in 2001) resurfacing and reconstruction of Santa Monica Boulevard has made the city's transit artery one of the world's most inviting.

IMAGES
*of America*

# WEST HOLLYWOOD

Ryan Gierach

ARCADIA
PUBLISHING

Published by Arcadia Publishing
Charleston, South Carolina


Library of Congress Catalog Card Number: 2003108754

For all general information contact Arcadia Publishing at:
Telephone 843-853-2070
Fax 843-853-0044
E-mail sales@arcadiapublishing.com
For customer service and orders:
Toll-Free 1-888-313-2665

Visit us on the Internet at www.arcadiapublishing.com

In the 1930s through the 1950s the world famous Sunset Strip helped to define the former rail yard as an international entertainment mecca to the stars. As this postcard from the 1970s shows, there was still glamour in abundance to be found along the Strip when rock and roll hit town.

# CONTENTS

Always at the cutting edge of design, the West Hollywood's Pacific Design Center has been a monumental testament to West Hollywood's forward-looking attitude. It anchors the vast West Hollywood Design District, an area of interior design shops and high-end furniture makers servicing the Beverly and Hollywood Hills, not to mention the Asian markets. The first blue building was built in the late 1970s, and the green tower in 1988. Recent change in ownership has made management more vigorous, resulting in new landscaping and massive sculptures like this one. A third and final eight-story maroon ovoid building is in the environmental impact stage at this writing.

# OVERVIEW

Once a no-man's-land, the couple square miles separating Beverly Hills and Los Angeles has become in the 21st century a veritable every-man's-land—the City of West Hollywood.

An 1850 surveyor called the future home of Los Angeles County's newest city "so desolate not even jackrabbits want to live there." Fast forward to 2003 and we find the one-time company town of Sherman sits at the rollicking center of Los Angeles night life. It is now Los Angeles' true creative core and is a mecca for progressive-minded and oppressed people from around the world. And, though the city is one of the most densely and diversely populated sections of the vast Los Angeles megalopolis, still nary a jackrabbit resides there to this day.

This image stands as West Hollywood's first history, just in time for the city's 20th birthday in 2004. I found as I studied history at UCLA that too many times other historians had conflated unincorporated West Hollywood and Los Angeles's Hollywood into one overarching idea of Super-Hollywood, and in the doing had co-opted, even stolen away, West Hollywood's singular story. This book is a humble attempt to begin setting that trend aright, but it is only just a beginning. Because of the format it is in no way meant to be anything but one historian's necessarily incomplete explanation, by way of available images, of how West Hollywood came to be a world-class entertainment and design center, not to mention a bastion of progressive politics.

Once upon a time, before the movies, West Hollywood was known as Sherman, a rough and tumble company town that grew up around a railroad yard and car barn. Next to Sherman were the newly discovered and developed Doheny and Gilmore oil fields. The citizens of the area were working-class immigrants, only a few with families, bringing a different approach to life than did their more temperate neighbors to the east in Hollywood. These men frequented bars, gambling halls, and brothels. They lived a life quite different from the sedate, middle-class neighbors in the nearby, and then-burgeoning, city of Hollywood.

Later, in the early days of Hollywood, West Hollywood sat at the center of the primarily Jewish movie industry. The captains of the movie industry (mostly Jewish immigrants) built inexpensive apartments by the dozens to house their extended families. The apartments began to fill with actors and people who dreamed of being actors, and thus was populated the Land of the Golden Reel.

The ruling county government barely noticed Sherman's existence, let alone that it was now being called West Hollywood, and the lack of oversight, law enforcement and building codes fostered the Wild West mentality of the town. It would remain a bohemian outpost well past Hollywood's hey-day, with speakeasies, gambling haunts, prostitution and massage parlors, bars and nightclubs, and drug joints supplying their services in an adult urban environment.

While rampant among the Hollywood stars, little of this seedy adult activity was in any way visible on the Strip above the tracks. Rather, glamour with a capital 'G' reigned on the Sunset

Strip. As actors and writers continued flocking to the West Hollywood Hills, their beloved "Strip" would be playground, office, and shopping destination. Still, the split personality of the town could be seen by looking down the hill, to Santa Monica Boulevard, where the rail yards still functioned and the tracks sang with freight trains and working class dreams.

Two cultural phenomena, rock and roll and television, came to town in a big way in the 1960s and 1970s, with studios just inside and outside the city cranking out the dramatic fare and music that filled the nation's radio and the television airwaves. The cheap rents made the area an important destination for the aspiring singers/actors/writers trying to make it onto a soap opera or break into the club scene. During this time, because Los Angeles County sheriff's deputies didn't harass gays as badly as did Los Angeles police officers, the unincorporated area of West Hollywood drew gays and lesbians to live there.

Upon gaining city status in 1984, West Hollywood attained its very own place in the sun as a municipality with an unlikely coalition of renters, seniors, Jews, and gays (this term, rather than the unwieldy Lesbian, Gay, Bisexual, and Transgender, will be used to denote non-heterosexuals throughout the book) who took control of their civic destinies. The shock waves that greeted incorporation reached around the world and resonate to this day, with rent control laws still being debated in the courts, and with gay rights issues holding sway in the culture wars that waft across the country and the Western world.

The new "Gay Camelot" titillated the world when twenty gay people chased five city council seats in 1984, with many asking if gays could run a city. However, history has a way of asking different questions, and the more pertinent question seems to be: Has city government improved municipal governance?

Because photos often came from multiple sources or archives, I have credited no photos. The list of resources I used for photos follows. Another point on the research should be made. Due to the format there is no bibliography, nor is there room to cite sources.

Many people helped in putting this project together. Thanks to the City of West Hollywood and Mayor Jeff Prang, council member John Heilman, Fran Solomon, and Helen Goss.

My main archivist, and the source for many of the historic photos, was Marc Wanamaker at Bison Archives, who is a dream to work with. Richard Settle, Gil Khan, Morris Kight (now deceased), Ron Andereg, Richard Stettles Miguel Angel Reyes, the Sherman Museum and Collection, Helen Levin, and the One Institute and Archives, thank you all for your submissions. Any recent photographs are mine.

To those for whom this book is a journey of discovery, I submit this story of how the most desolate place on the planet became arguably the most creative spot on Earth.

# One

# RANCHO LA BREA

The region that West Hollywood inhabits enjoys one of the finest climates on earth, generally sunny, warm, and dry, with moderate winter rainfall and dry summers. This is a climate found on only three percent of the world's land surface. Los Angeles County stretches in a coastal plain for 40 miles from the mountains named the San Gabriel to the hills of Palos Verdes. The lifeblood of this semi-desert region is water and, until 1913, the irregular flow of the Los Angeles and San Gabriel Rivers provided the only outside source. Prior to the arrival of the Spaniards little activity stirred the peaceful aridity of the plain, and animals came to drink in the dark pools of the La Brea Tar Pits. This view is from the hillside that protects West Hollywood (then called Sherman) from the north, and points south toward the Baldwin Hills and the ocean beyond.

The deep human history of the area containing West Hollywood lies in that area just to the south of it: the La Brea Tar Pits. Aboriginal Americans used the pitch and tar they found bubbling to the surface there to be useful for waterproofing. Because of the tar bubbling to the surface, the land area was useless for the Indians, except for the pitch or the occasional trapped animal they were able to snare. However, water did gather on top of the asphalt, providing a fresh supply in an arid land. Only much later did European settlers think to drill for and make use of the oil that the asphalt indicated lay beneath the surface.

Tar pits are actually springs of molten asphaltum, or asphalt, which is a residual form of petroleum. Since the Pleistocene Epoch, commonly known as the "Ice Age," various mammals, birds, reptiles, and organic matter have been trapped in the deep, viscous swamps of asphalt, ultimately submerging and dying. The animals were invariably trapped when they sought the water that is so scarce in these parts, and others were trapped because they attempted to capture already trapped animals. The large number of scavengers recovered in digs testifies to that fact.

Passing through the area abutting the Santa Monica Mountains to reach the Cahuenga Pass on his original trip through the area in January 1770, the first Europeans to see Southern California, those with Governor Gaspar de Portolá's expeditionary force, paused near West Hollywood and the tar pits to say mass and avail themselves of the pitch to waterproof their equipment and clothing. It was just the year before, in 1769, that the first Spanish effort to settle Southern California was made with San Gabriel Mission. In 1781 a civil town named Los Angeles grew up along the banks of the Los Angeles River, begun by 44 people in 11 families. In 1822, when Mexico gained its independence from Spain, ranchos were given out to close associates of the governor. Native Americans were made virtual slaves to the Catholic missionaries.

After the Spaniards "tamed" the Gabrielano Indians through Catholicism and the missions, and Mexico gained its independence, the 'Alcade,' or local governor, of Los Angeles parceled out ranches to his stalwart friends in the 1830s and 1840s. Rancho La Brea eventually became Hollywood, West Hollywood, and Hancock Park, and Rancho De Las Aguas became West Hollywood, Beverly Hills, and Beverlywood. The owners of the ranchos seldom lived on the land, leaving the adobe houses they were mandated to build within a year of their land grants to their major domos, or ranch managers. These men oversaw the cattle trade that made up the only industry in the entire area. Cattle was the main source of income for the Southern California ranchos. Herds of cattle were abundant and allowed to roam the wide open plains, hills, and canyons in the pastoral days of the rancho.

Smallpox and other Western viral agents wiped out the Gabrielanos in the mid-1800s. Missions owned more cattle and tallow manufactories than the pueblo and the rancheros combined. Cattle and easily-transported by-products, such as hide and candles, were the region's only commerce. The missions were secularized from 1834–1836, and ranchos were created from their lands. Drought in 1860s destroyed cattle as a way of life, throwing open the lands to development and, as the railroad joined the basin to the rest of the country, tremendous growth.

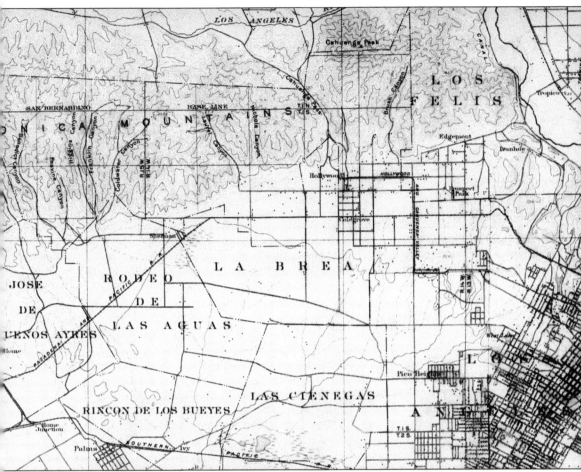

Rancho La Brea was granted to Antonio Jose Rocha and Nemisio Dominguez by Jose Antonio Carrillo, the alcade of Los Angeles in 1828. It consisted of one square league of land (4,439 acres) along what is today Wilshire Boulevard and included the land to the north, including today's West Hollywood and Hollywood, up to the mountains where Sunset Boulevard runs now. When the United States conquered California, the fighting was sharp and fierce. Mexican General Andres Pico capitulated to Lt. Col. John C. Fremont near the Cahuenga Pass on January 13, 1847, handing California over to the Americans.

After the United States took California from Mexico in the Mexican-American War the lands were surveyed by a Maj. Henry Hancock, whose expertise came into play in proving the Rancho La Brea owners' claim to their land. However, the legal battle left the ranchero broke and eager to hand over the rancho to Hancock to pay the bills for his consultancy. Hancock began to make commercial use of the tar fields, building a refinery in the 1850 to sell tar and asphalt to Los Angeles and San Francisco. The Hancock family controlled most of the Rancho through the oil boom of the 1880s and 1890s. Oil discovered and pumped from the areas of West Hollywood and La Brea made the Hancocks one of the wealthiest of California families. The subdivision known as Hancock Park carries their name, the exclusive Wilshire Country Club (est. 1920) their imprimatur.

George Caralambo, a Turk of Greek descent who later changed his name to Allen, was selected by the United States' Camel Corps to lead "a pack of camels hauling supplies to build the Butterfield Overland Stage Route from St. Louis" to Los Angeles in 1855. Hancock, who met him as part of their mutual military service, built a stable and house for "Greek George" and his camels on a bet that the stage route could be used as a dromedary mail run. The route died without active support of the military, and Greek George was forced to 'liberate' his animals, some of which wandered the neighborhood for 30 years after. Greek George, who was quite a musician and bon vivant, stayed on at the stables to care for Hancock's cattle and horses, becoming a naturalized American citizen in 1867.

Tiburcio Vasquez, pictured at bottom, center, a two-time federal prisoner and feared highwayman, had, since 1870, raided and sacked several whole towns, leaving three dead in one. A $15,000 bounty was placed on his head in 1874 by the state legislature. William R. Rowland, sheriff of Los Angeles County, plotted long to capture Vasquez while he holed up in the hills at Kings Road and Santa Monica with Greek George and conducted audacious robberies. Greek George was downtown supposedly seeking information on the sheriff's doings, leaving his wife and baby with the outlaw and one of his men. The other bandits were up in the hills. Vasquez was captured in a shoot-out and promptly arrested and taken to Los Angeles for questioning and trial. His capture was a celebrated event. A burlesque troupe at the Merced Theater performed a take-off on his career and capture in the days following. Vasquez' capture symbolizes the wild west beginnings of the area. Greek George took the reward money and moved away.

The Wild West that Los Angeles had been was being tamed by Midwestern transplants during the Reconstruction Era. As this wave of immigrants settled in and developed Hollywood they brought a blend of agriculture, churches, and temperance. Reform was in the air and the "bad man" was no longer welcome in Los Angeles, least of all in Hollywood. Not least among the new buildings in Los Angeles and its neighbor towns were churches of several denominations. The rancho life was giving way to the farmer's life, and in their quiet way, the decent men, women, and children who brought these institutions with them to a rough-hewn land were crowding out the desperados of Los Angeles.

# Two

# SHERMAN,
# COMPANY TOWN

The history of Los Angeles, city and county, is written in large part by transportation systems, both without and within. Each major development: the building of the Southern Pacific and Santa Fe Railways, the local inter-urban lines, the electric transit systems, and shipping routes to the harbors, shaped the growth and character of the area. The completion of, and the ensuing rate competition between the two railways, Southern Pacific and Santa Fe, brought about a land boom of the 1880s by bringing Midwesterners to the area in droves. The Southern Pacific Railroad's opening in 1883 drove fares as low as one dollar between Kansas City and Los Angeles. Land sales to Midwesterners skyrocketed to $13 million a month.

Moses Sherman, pictured here on the left of Sheriff Bill Hammel and his brother-in-law, Eli P. Clark, dominated the Los Angeles street railroad scene for two decades, the last of the 19th and the first of the 20th centuries. The pair would later partner with Henry Huntington in the creation of a railroad system that would tie the disparate pieces of the Los Angeles basin into a whole. Sherman chose the spot midway between downtown and the beach for his rail yard and station on the famous "Balloon Route" that carried passengers from downtown to Santa Monica and then to Redondo Beach and back downtown again. Up around the yards grew a small village of shop workers, supervisors, and conductors that Sherman named for himself.

The first trolley built in Los Angeles was Col. C.H. Howland's Pico Heights in 1887, which delivered homeowners to their doors. Sherman built his first line from downtown to Pasadena and out to the beach in 1890. Later Henry E. Huntington expanded Sherman's operations to include 73 other railways into the Pacific Electric Railway Company, which ran the "Red Cars" until 1941. In 1899 Henry E. Huntington, son of Collis of SP notoriety, and partners, embarked on the creation of the Pacific Electric Railway. Sherman was a partner by virtue of his line, the Los Angeles Railway.

With love and affection
To General Sherman
on his Seventy first
Birthday.

Sherman was tall, 6' 9", with a lantern jaw and demeanor and stance which demanded attention. He exuded unbound optimism and had a particular skill in distancing money from investors' pockets. Born in 1853 in Vermont, he first taught school until health problems sent him in search of desert air in Arizona. Within time he was superintendent of schools for the territory. He invested in land, formed a bank, and took over the city's tiny horse-car system of trolleys. His sister married Clark in 1876 and they electrified the Phoenix trolley system in 1893. He was a master at borrowing money to finance his schemes and "could charm a bird right out of a tree," according to accounts. Sherman was intimately involved with Harry Chandler in building the HollywoodLand development. He was sitting on the Water Board when several of his and Chandler's friends bought up the San Fernando Valley in advance of the announcement of the Owens Lake project and the planned building of a new aqueduct. He gave his own name to Sherman Oaks in the deal.

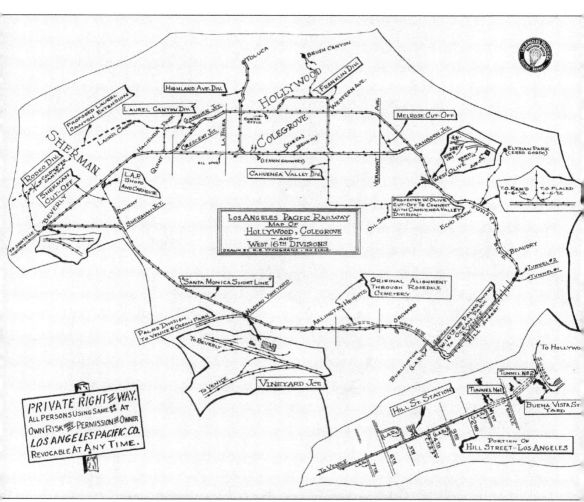

Sherman and Clark quickly entered the railway fray in Los Angeles. Sherman, as owner of the soon-to-be-defunct Pasadena and Pacific Railroad, bought the corner of Santa Monica and San Vicente in 1896 for his headquarters, car barn, shop, and power station. He reorganized in 1898 as the Los Angeles-Pacific Railroad Company, taking over the car barn and line again and calling the complex and the surrounding community of railway workers "Sherman." Eventually the Los Angeles-Pacific Railroad had over 250 miles of narrow gauge track spreading from downtown into the valley at Burbank and out to the sea at Santa Monica. The stops included Prospect Park (Hollywood), Wynetka (Beverly Hills), Cahuenga (Hollywood), Colegrove (Hollywood), Hammel and Denker (an ostrich ranch), and Soldiers' Home (Westwood). Running at speeds of up to 55 miles per hour, the trolleys delivered people to their jobs and home again in beach cities like Long Beach, Redondo Beach, and Venice. Weekend enthusiasts rode the car to various beach destinations, disembarking several times before making the circuit home.

Sherman built the Sherman station, yards, car barns, and shops in 1896 on 5.6 acres of land. He laid two and a half miles of yard tracks and built a steam power house and a shop building. The area in back of, and below, the Sherman Yards was swampland, so Sherman filled the area. A parade of dirt trains brought dirt from the Sunset cuts and filled in an additional 14 acres on which Sherman built more buildings and an eventual total of six and a half miles of track. The Los Angeles-Pacific Railroad ran ubiquitous Green Cars to the beach, the valley, and through Hollywood, which makes it " . . . safe to say that LAP caused the beach population to double inside of five years," as Luther Ingersoll wrote in *Century History of Santa Monica*.

The buildings contained therein were a blacksmith shop, a brass foundry, an iron foundry, two car houses, a car repair shop, an oil house, storehouses and a power house (changed over to a substation in 1905). By 1911, J.M. Guinn, a Los Angeles historian, was saying about the Rancho that had been since forgotten, "Time, flood, and the hated gringo have long since obliterated all ancient landmarks and boundary lines of the old pueblo."

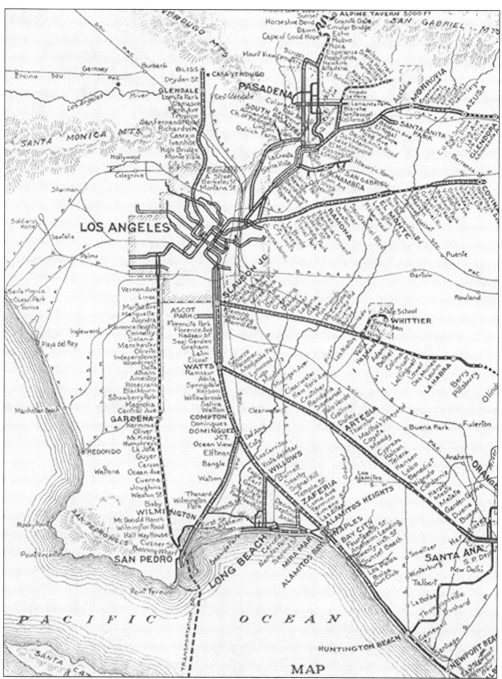

MAP

In 1906 the Southern Pacific, headed by E.H. Harriman, secured control of the LAP from Sherman and Clark by buying a majority stake. Sherman and Clark were left in control, and vast sums were infused to improve the lines. The pair retired in 1910, while the town around the plant and car barn remained Sherman for a decade more. Their retirement also set off a great set of electric rail mergers forced by Harriman that resulted in the creation of the Pacific Electric system, the Red Cars. This system dominated the transportation scene until after World War I. It ran as passenger rail until 1954 and freight rode the rails until 1961.

The Laurel School District built a school at Laurel and Sunset in 1886. In 1890 the Methodist Episcopal Church South built a church at Fairfax and Santa Monica, but moved shortly into Hollywood. Shortly after Los Angeles annexed Hollywood the area above Laurel Canyon became a popular scenic spot, with a mountain-top inn and bungalows with views being built in 1910 and 1911. Lookout Mountain Inn had 24 rooms, a bandstand, a pavilion, and a restaurant with a 270 degree view of Los Angeles. The restaurant served a chicken dinner specialty as a reward for the 45 minute drive up the steep grade. Bungalowland accompanied the inn, and to increase interest in the homes developers built a trolley that ran up and down the canyon on the half hour for six years. The Laurel Canyon line ran on Sunset from Gardner Junction to Laurel Canyon Boulevard from 1884, for nearly one mile. It was electrified in 1905, with through service to Los Angeles (a 40 minute trip) added in 1907. The Inn burned in 1918 and the trolley closed soon after. The tracks were removed in 1930.

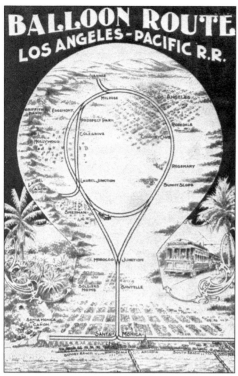

The Balloon Route Trolley Trip was the most famous trolley trip in the west. In its day, few tourists to Los Angeles missed riding the Balloon Route cars. The excursion consisted of as many as 18 cars daily going from the downtown to Hollywood to visit artist Paul DeLongpre's house; then on to Soldiers' Home for a picture on the steps, the photographer taking a regular car back to the studio, developing the photos, rejoining the group and selling the prints to the passengers; then on the Santa Monica's Long Wharf. "They got a kick out of that," said C.M. Pierce himself, "We said it was the only ocean voyage in the world on wheels—and never any seasickness."

Pierce once said, "I can hear those spielers now: 'Balloon Route Excursion—not up in the air but down on the earth.' The scenic trolley trip, goes one way and returns another. A hundred and one miles for a hundred cents. One whole day for a dollar. Thirty-six miles right along the ocean shore. The only way to see it and see it right." The Camera Obscura and the Ocean Park Bathhouse in Santa Monica was next, followed by a dinner stop, ice skating, and/or boat rides in the lagoon in Playa Del Rey. Afterwards the cars would stop at Redondo Beach in a search for moonstones. Then Venice for an hour, to allow canal-gazing and shopping, and then a fast run home. The trip back downtown through Palms took only 20 minutes. The excursion's heyday lasted until 1911 when S&P took over excursions. Pierce's enthusiasm found expression in other tours, but the Balloon Route suffered ignominious neglect and eventual death.

Red Cars brought workers to the bean fields of West Hollywood and Beverly Hills. The South Hollywood-Sherman Line was Los Angeles Pacific's first line, built by Pasadena & Pacific and taken over by Sherman when the newer company was formed, went through Sherman in 1895, and was completed to the beach in Santa Monica in 1896. Although many agricultural workers lived on the land they cared for, seasonal help would use the trolleys to come and go during harvest or planting at these large farms. Trolleys ran 30 and more times a day back and forth between downtown and the beach. However, the route became congested with the growth of Hollywood and travelers began using cars. The trip, which once took 35 minutes by train but, by the 1930s took 90 minutes, could be completed in only 40 minutes in an automobile.

The St. Victor's Catholic Church structure was donated by Belgium businessman and neighbor Victor Ponet. Ponet thought the mostly Catholic Mexicans were in danger of backsliding for lack of a convenient church, and wanted the railway workers to be attending mass instead of drinking alcohol on Sunday mornings. His donation of the land and the building was rewarded by the church's carrying his patron saint's name, St. Victor, thus becoming the first church dedicated to the 13th pope. The building was dedicated on December 5, 1906. The congregation used a priest from the parish in Hollywood. A new church was built in 1960. The arrival of the priest from nearby Blessed Sacrament for Sunday mass in Sherman was always a sight: with Moses Sherman's personal rail car screaming to a halt in a billowing dust cloud, the black and red and white priestly robes fluttering in the wind as the hillside church bells peeled in glad announcement of his arrival, and his ascendance into the Ponet family carriage, and then his winding ascent up the hill being pulled by two glistening stallions to disembark on the wide sun-washed church-step overlook.

In addition to the rail yard and the church the town had a handful of taverns, one brothel, and a few score homes for the workers at the oil field and yard. By 1919 Sherman was a collection of scattered roads and large grain fields. The area bounded by Beverly, La Brea, Sunset, and Doheny was, at this time, considered to be West Hollywood.

L.J. Quint had the only general store in Sherman, the only business to service the nearby residents of Sherman in Sherman for years. He was also the postmaster. Soon, the area became known as a destination for homeowners who especially liked the hillside homes. Next door, Hollywood had already become a city unto its own when this photo was taken, but would decide that re-joining Los Angeles might provide the new agricultural community with access to water. Hollywood ceased to be a city in 1910. In 1924, when annexation to the city of Los Angeles seemed beneficial to those in Sherman, a hard-fought referendum lost out by a bare majority, 814 votes to 750. From 1919 on the town was called both West Hollywood and Sherman, causing some confusion, but by 1925 the townsfolk universally were using the more glamorous West Hollywood.

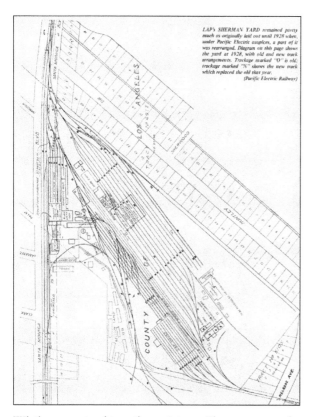

LAP's SHERMAN YARD *remained pretty much as originally laid out until 1928 when, under Pacific Electric auspices, a part of it was rearranged. Diagram on this page shows the yard at 1928, with old and new track arrangements. Trackage marked "O" is old; trackage marked "N" shows the new track which replaced the old that year.*
*(Pacific Electric Railway)*

While operating his railway, Moses Sherman served on the Board of Water Commissioners at the time that Fred Eaton and William Mulholland bought the rights to the Owens Valley water and designed an aqueduct to Los Angeles in the 1910s. Sherman secretly gave that information to business associates who had then preemptively bought up the San Fernando Valley in anticipation of the secret move. Sherman and his cronies got very rich very fast when the water began to flow, a much needed boost to Sherman's fortunes, because in the 1920s the fixed transit system went into decline, in part the victim of its own success. Rail spread communities across the Los Angeles basin, but it was the automobile which helped develop the previously predominantly agricultural San Fernando Valley. Sherman Oaks is named for Moses Sherman. Pictured below Sherman at right is Eli Clark.

Moses H. Sherman

Sherman Foundation

# *Three*

# COMPANY TOWN OF THE STARS!

In 1906 Sherman was a rail yard surrounded by the company's workers' houses, which were surrounded by fields of grain, with scattered roads running nowhere over nothing, except for the farm fields that tumbled down the hillside for as far as the eyes could discern. The workers labored in grease and grime to cart passengers and freight. They lived loudly in their bars and quietly in their houses. However, the area known as Sherman, bounded by Beverly, La Brea, Sunset, and Doheny, was about to take on a new name, and with it, a whole new identity, within just a generation.

The Hancock family controlled most of Rancho La Brea through the oil boom of the 1880s and 1890s. Oil discovered and pumped from the area of West Hollywood and La Brea made the Hancocks one of the wealthiest of California families. The subdivision known as Hancock Park carries their name; the exclusive Wilshire Country Club, (est. 1920) their imprimatur. Excavation of the La Brea Tar Pits brought up evidence of its archeological value when, in 1913, Mrs. Ida Hancock gave 13 acres of pits to the county for archeological investigation. That act formed the basis for today's George C. Page Museum. Found in the pits were the Imperial Elephant, or Mastodon, standing 15 feet high (as compared to today's elephant's reach of 11 feet), little ground sloths, prehistoric camels, California horses, many saber-tooth tigers, and assorted small mammals such as antelope, peccary, pigs, skunks, and weasels.

Arthur Gilmore purchased a small western and northern section of Rancho La Brea where West Hollywood joins Beverly Hills and Los Angeles in the 1880s for a dairy farm. He struck oil drilling for water for his cows in 1903. He saw the value in the oil, especially with the new automobile being built. He formed the A.F. Gilmore Oil Company, which funded development of the area immediately adjacent to West Hollywood, including Farmer's Market, Gilmore Field, and later CBS Studios. Edward L. Doheny, who had struck oil downtown in 1882, quickly bought land just to the north in West Hollywood and sank wells. He was to become the very richest of all California oilmen. The area would become spined with oil derricks, and oil production in the immediate vicinity would continue into the 21st century.

It was a different kind of gold that brought change to the area: celluloid gold, the movie industry. These changes would make West Hollywood a bastion of progressive politics and draw refugees from the world over. In the early days of the 20th century a number of mostly Jewish film makers and producers descended upon the area to make motion pictures. Most of them came to the area because it was beyond the reach of the Edison patent lawyers whom they were cheating, and by whom they were being sued. Director D.W. Griffith wore a gun at his side while he worked, and not because rattlesnakes dotted the landscape. He was known to shoot at people resembling process-servers.

The filming of movies started in Los Angeles as early as 1907. Beginning in 1916 movies were made in West Hollywood. Triangle Film Company filmed *Casey at the Bat* at Sherman Field, a baseball field that stands to this day. Union Film Company, Sherman's first permanent (if such can be said of any film company in those days) film producers made films at their Hammond Street and Santa Monica Boulevard location beginning in 1920. Beginning at the turn of the century, the area bounded by Poinsettia and Seward and by Willoughby and Fountain (just next to the soon-to-be opened Pickford Fairbank studios) was designated as industrial or light industrial. There were plating factories (still operating in 2003), movie studios, welders, mechanics, etc. located on this swath of land. This gave the east end of town a decidedly working-class cast, quite a contrast from the high-end residential Crescent Heights and Harper Avenue apartment districts which grew up to house actors and writers.

Jesse D. Hampton, tobacco executive turned film-maker, built the Jesse D. Hampton Studios with a mammoth stage and back lot at Formosa and Santa Monica Boulevard in 1919. The same year, Charlie Chaplin Studios were built within blocks of Hampton's, one just inside and the other just outside of Hollywood proper. Just two years later the studio expanded and added Pickford Fairbanks Studios. Mary Pickford, America's Sweetheart, and Douglas Fairbanks, the most dashing leading man in Hollywood, would create one of the most successful, and stable, motion picture studios in town, filming *Thief of Baghdad* and other action blockbusters on the back lot in West Hollywood. They would eventually join with others to create United Artists.

Samuel Goldwyn, a Polish-born Jew by way of New York, impacted peoples' lives with his films like no other in Hollywood's Golden Age of the 1930s. With new friends Louis B. Mayer and Jessie Lasky, he moved to (West) Hollywood to reign over one of the most successful studios in town. He left Metro Goldwyn Mayer (MGM) and took up residence at United Artists (UA) in 1924. Eventually he became a partner, and then president in 1931, and then changed the studio's name to Goldwyn Studios after buying out Pickford, Chaplin, and Fairbanks. He finally took over the lot from his partners in 1955 in a highly visible court battle. He brought to UA his Ronald Coleman unit, along with Vilma Banky and Gary Cooper and directors George Fitzmaurice and Henry King. This team, and the UA studios under Goldwyn's direction and leadership, would become a Hollywood powerhouse studio with such blockbusters as *The Black Pirate* and *The Man in the Iron Mask* starring Douglas Fairbanks.

William S. Hart, gentleman Western star, lived in West Hollywood just beneath Sunset Boulevard at 8135 DeLongpre while he was Hollywood's third highest paid star, behind Chaplin and Pickford, making $17,000 a week. Hart, Fairbanks, Pickford, and Chaplin were all friends. When the idea for United Artists came up, Hart alone of the group resisted. Hart was an oddity in youth-oriented Hollywood: he was 50 years old when he made his start in the movies. He felt too old to be forming studios. D.W. Griffith, however, came in from outside to make a fourth. Hart retreated to his Newhall ranch and left his house to the City of Los Angeles after his death. In later years the city of West Hollywood took possession of the property, which is used as a park and educational facility.

Meanwhile, screen vamp Alla Nazimova, an open lesbian and radical bohemian who enjoyed a reign as the most popular actress of the silent film era, built the Garden of Allah in 1921. It was built just inside West Hollywood at 8150 Sunset Boulevard on the corner of Crescent Heights and Sunset Boulevard. Of interest to Nazimova, whose frankly licentious and bawdy behavior made her disinterested in overmuch law enforcement, the residence hotel, built in fabulous splendor, was just outside the City of Los Angeles and the prying eyes of the Los Angeles Police. Nazimova gloried in her ability to shock and offend, inviting a large mix of people to the hotel for avant-garde parties where she could display her friends' debaucheries and enjoy the look of frank disapproval on the faces of up-tight guests. The grand-opening party boasted troubadours playing madrigals from the middle of the swimming pool, and 18 hours worth of celebration with food and drink for all the biggest stars in Hollywood. The hotel bar and studio apartments saw the likes of Frank Sinatra, Bing Crosby, Lana Turner, F. Scott Fitzgerald, Ramon Navarro, Errol Flynn, Tallulah Bankhead, and Clara Bow. Visitors also included people like Mickey Cohen, who was known to be in the mob. The hotel's seedy reputation soon caught up with it and the stars no longer wished to be seen there by the late 1940s.

A highly illuminating incident described by mobster Mickey Cohen indicates the high level of mob-to-star shoulder rubbing. "On Benny's orders," said Cohen, (Benny was Bugsy Siegel's preferred name—nobody called him Bugsy to his face), "I went into this private club and raised the joint. I had the shotgun on everybody. I was watching this good-looking lady and the guy with her. Goddamn, she was beautiful. I knew she was a movie person. But who the hell was she? We got the dough and the jewelry and we took off." Two years later, after Cohen had moved higher up the mob ladder, he was at a party, again in Hollywood, when he looked up and saw this little "blonde casing me and whispering something to Florabel Muir, the *New York Daily Hollywood* columnist." Florabel walked over to Cohen and said, "Mickey, do you remember that little lady over there?" Cohen said, "Yeah, that's a movie star." "That's Betty Grable," Muir answered. "Yeah, you met her before, you took her jewelry." The Garden saw glamour and wild parties to be sure, but it also saw its share of robbery, murder, drunkenness, despair, loneliness, orgies, marriages, mistresses and divorces, pranks, fights, and tragic suicides. Nazimova went bust during the Depression and the building hobbled on in a hotel dotage until it began to fall down around the occupants' heads in the late 1940s. It was re-developed into a bank and shopping center in the early 1950s. It could be said that, since a McDonald's has been built on the grounds, the earth beneath the Garden of Allah has been salted like the soils of Carthage.

Movies brought incredible growth to Hollywood, an area defined as the land between Beverly Boulevard and the summit of the Hollywood Hills at the intersection of Doheny Drive and Hoover. Between 1910 and 1920 the population grew from 5,000 to 36,000. There was a 6.5 times increase in the next decade to 235,000 people. In those twenty years agriculture was abandoned completely for business supporting the film industry and housing. In the second photo, the back lot at Pickford Fairbanks Studio is being prepared for the filming of the *Thief of Baghdad*. Entire 'cities' were built on that lot and torn down again to make room for more sets, keeping the local lumber yards and carpenters very busy.

The industrial quality of the Santa Monica Boulevard main drag continued to develop with the Mitchell Camera Company building a massive factory just off Santa Monica Boulevard on Robertson next to the rail yard in 1929. Mitchell produced most of the still and motion picture cameras used by the industry in the day. On the other side of the unincorporated town stood Pickford Fairbanks Studios, Chaplin Studios, Famous Players-Lasky Studio, and Union Studio, churning out film after film with Mitchell's cameras. The building is still in use today, but as a disco. The other photo shows the front office of Mary Pickford Company at Formosa Gate one half block south of Santa Monica Boulevard.

The Sunset Strip, officially nonexistent on any map or record, began as a wagon trail to the ocean and the mountainside passes, Laurel, Cahuenga, Benedict, and Coldwater. Prohibition affected West Hollywood only in that, to the nouveau riche of Tinsel Town, they relied now on speakeasies beginning to line the Strip rather than the 'lounges,' the pseudonym for bars. Drugs such as cocaine, ether, and marijuana, not yet illegal, found favor among the new Hollywood stars through the Roaring Twenties. Drug peddlers and rum runners, pimps and hit men, gamblers and conmen, all flourished in the lawless environment of West Hollywood, especially along the Sunset Strip. It was this combination of stars and starlets seeking freedom to play, and the speakeasies eagerness to help them out, that transformed the Sunset Strip in the 1920s and 1930s from farm road to playground for the stars. In 1924 commercial buildings began springing up along the hillside strip of road, such as Sunset Towers in 1928. The year this aerial photo was taken, 1926, Sherman voted to take advantage of its world-famous neighbor by calling itself West Hollywood.

In the 1920s residence hotels like the Chateau Marmont and Sunset Towers were built to accommodate the new stars' need for housing. The Montgomery family developed its stretch of the Strip into Sunset Plaza, a high end shopping destination for the new Hollywood rich. Chateau Marmont boasted that all of the famous names in entertainment stayed there at one time or another. Billy Wilder, Jean Harlow, Greta Garbo, Boris Karloff, Howard Hughes, and Marilyn Monroe top the list. The stars particularly valued the privacy offered in the Chateau's bungalows.

Ciro's, Mocambo, Trocadero, names that will ring forever in the lore of Hollywood, all sported top name draws in the Strip's heyday in the 30s and 40s, with the Troc's Nat King Cole Trio installed in its own room, Xavier Cugat at Ciro's, and Hazel Scott playing piano boogie at Mocambo. A strict policy prohibiting unaccompanied singles and couples of the same sex kept the places hopping. Often women would appear on the arm of a male friend or friends, or vice versa, but would invariably leave on the arm of someone they'd met inside. The boundaries of sexuality blurred within the walls of these clubs, with several of the entertainers doing what can only be described as "camp," and even some drag. The gay actors and actresses who were photographed arriving with those of the opposite sex were invariably glad to find the photographers missing at the end of the night when they departed with a person of the same sex.

Mocambo opened in 1939 by Charles Morrison, and quickly became the movie stars' haunt. The club closed in 1958 after Morrison's death. The tolerance for bending gender and sexual roles in this and other Sunset Strip clubs also gave the "creative" performers a chance to stretch their material to fit the more adult tastes of the crowds without attracting the attention of the Los Angeles Police just a few blocks away. Mob activity was tolerated as well. Al Capone visited West Hollywood in 1927 and was welcomed with open arms by the moguls, mostly Jewish. His lieutenants, Bugsy Siegel and Mickey Cohen among them, stayed at the Gardens of Allah, along with F. Scott Fitzgerald, Norma Talmadge, and Jean Harlow. In the 1930s Willie Bioff

and George Brown, men with underworld ties, moved into the top ranks of the International Alliance of Theatrical Stage Employees and Moving Picture Operators (IATSE), threatened a projectionists strike and extorted payments from the studios in the six figures. The bribes were first delivered to Bioff at the Garden of Allah's bar. Crime figures rubbed shoulders with the Hollywood crowd regularly in the " . . . luxurious restaurants and night clubs, coffee shops and all-night sandwich joints, not to mention false-fronted gambling spots, casinos, drug hangouts, steam baths, massage parlors, bordellos and burlesque houses."

The Garden of Allah, the Chateau Marmont, and the other beginnings of the Sunset Strip attracted small shops and lunch counters. Schwabs, made famous when used as a location in Billy Wilder's *Sunset Boulevard* in 1950, became *the* watering hole and place to see and be seen for agents directors and stars. Wilder was living at the Chateau Marmont at the time of filming. Publicist and producer Sidney Skolosky used Schwabs as his office, and Groucho Marx kept an office across the street but held court at Schwabs' lunch counter. Mickey Cohen, mob associate of Bugsy Siegel's, ran a bookie parlor from his otherwise innocent-appearing haberdashery on Sunset very near Schwabs. For decades aspiring stars and starlets dined at Schwabs' lunch counter hoping to be discovered.

Director Preston Sturges had a series of hits in the late 1930s and very early 1940s. He did not care for the food at Chasen's or Musso and Franks Grill, the two places in which to "be seen" in Hollywood, so he opened the three-story Players Club on the Strip below the Chateau Marmont. It had drive-up service on the ground, informal dining on the second floor, and formal coat-and-tie dining on the third floor overlooking the Los Angeles basin from its hillside aerie. The cost of opening the restaurant was an astounding $250,000 and the restaurant would eventually cost Sturges everything he had. While it was open the club became a major draw for the movie and arts crowd on the Strip, which itself reigned supreme as America's adult entertainment destination until Las Vegas was built in the early 1950s.

Movie studios through the 1930s created something of a cartel in West Hollywood, controlling their mostly non-union employees with an iron fist and controlling local businesses' fates with their checkbooks. This control over wages and prices kept both low; the lack of municipal government meant that landlords and businesses could cut corners and costs with impunity. The lax oversight on land use in the area led to the building of scores of cheap-looking businesses (especially those standing along the railway on Santa Monica) and tawdry apartments. This photo, taken just a few blocks beneath the Sunset Strip, show how West Hollywood had something of a split architectural personality. However, that architectural bi-polar disorder also meant that architects with dreams could give them full expression.

Rudolf Michael Schindler was born in 1887 in Vienna, Austria. He studied both art and architecture before joining architect Frank Lloyd Wright in Los Angeles. In 1920 he supervised the construction of Wright's Hollyhock House. Rudolf M. Schindler's home was the first modern house to respond to the unique climate of California, and as such it served as the prototype for a distinctly Californian style of design. From 1922 until his death in 1953, the building functioned as Schindler's house and studio. During this 30-year period, Schindler, often partnering with boyhood friend Richard Nuetra, designed houses and small commercial buildings that today are considered landmarks of the modern movement. R.M. Schindler built his house on Kings Road in 1922 after a camping trip led him to envision creating an outdoor feeling to an enclosed space. This 3,400 square feet home wasn't intended for living in, it was intended as a prototype. Schindler compared it to a camper's shelter with a solid back, and an open front like a tent flap, which were the sliding canvass doors. "The real rooms of the house are out of doors," said Kathryn Smith, one-time tenant and restoration fund-raiser about the house. Schindler and his wife Pauline were free spirits of the Roaring Twenties, wearing flowing costumes and all cotton clothing that tied rather than buttoned. They threw all-night parties at their then nearly isolated home. Other tenants in the Schindler House included Galka Scheyker, the American agent for European artists Vassily Kandinsky and Paul Klee.

The successes of Goldwyn, Schenk, Schindler, and Nuetra in America gave hope to other progressives and Jews living in Europe before World War II. Soon a flow of Jews escaping Nazism and fascism, many of them artists, writers, and musicians, came to West Hollywood, laying down a path to freedom which would be trod tens of thousands of times. These photos show that not only was the film industry eager to utilize the newcomers, but there was space for housing as well. Still, every refugee carried fear in his suitcase. Fear of unemployment, of ostracism in a new land, of hunger, disgrace, fear, and even of retribution from the evil regime they just left. Composer Arnold Schoenberg, who had emigrated from Germany, wrote his son from sunny and bright Los Angeles, "Something very important: Don't say anything you don't have to say about your experiences of the last few weeks. . . . You know the Nazis take revenge on relatives and friends still in their power."

Anti-Jewish sentiment could be found in Los Angeles as well in the 1930s and 1940s. Jewish movie studio executives were not free to live where they pleased, thus the areas south and west of Hollywood, such as Beverly Hills, the west side of West Hollywood, and Beverlywood saw concentrations of wealthier Jews. The Hacienda Arms (1927), shown here, was one of the finest residences in its day. It was later used as a private gambling casino for the stars. The Casa Granada (1929), left, is another example of high-end housing built for the movie people of any religious stripe. All were tolerated, explaining perhaps why so few stars lived in Hollywood proper and so many lived on unincorporated Los Angeles county land named West Hollywood.

For all the glamour up the hill on or just beneath the Strip, the Santa Monica Boulevard corridor retained its decidedly working-class cast with trolley and freight cars making regular runs down the center of that street. Unregulated lumber yards, hardware stores, welders, auto mechanics, and dry cleaners flourished while they threw out grime, dust, and noxious smells into the air.

This large dairy complex south of the LAP rail yards sits on a site straddling Los Angeles and West Hollywood in 1928 that is now occupied by Cedars-Sinai Hospital. The Hospital was built with Jewish entertainment money and made famous by its many celebrity patients. The photo also shows the continued dominance over the area that the Sherman Rail yards enjoyed. That massive area would be redeveloped later to hold a bus depot, a sheriff's station, and the Pacific Design Center.

# MONTGOMERY PROPERTIES, LTD.

PIONEERS IN THE SUNSET STRIP

8623 SUNSET BOULEVARD

LOS ANGELES

A Few Locations Available

for Select Shops

Up the hill directly above the dairy sat Montgomery Holdings, the basis for a 20th century real estate empire focused along the Strip and in the West Hollywood Hills. The Montgomery family would play an important role in the city's development, and would become the most ardent foe of incorporation in the 1980s. Their Sunset Plaza development formed the core of the Sunset Strip, rivaling nearby and world-famous shopping districts such as Beverly Hills' Rodeo Drive, and Hollywood and Vine.

52

This was where the stars hung out in the 1930s. As film actors frequented the shops along the Strip, such as Elizabeth Arden's pictured here, the Montgomery Family's Sunset Plaza outdoor mall quickly became the world's most glamorous shopping destination. The finest in haute couture, lunch, or a fine dinner and a cocktail could be had on what was a few years earlier a dirt farm road. The view of the Los Angeles basin was splendid, as one could easily see the ocean and Palos Verdes on clear days. Most of the original buildings of the Plaza still exist. As the aerial view shows, a densely populated city of apartment buildings grew up around this hub of shopping and entertainment. The Sunset Strip can be seen near the top of the picture wiggling roughly southwest below the hills. Santa Monica Boulevard is the straight gash turning south and west in the center. One can spot the Sherman Rail Yards in the bottom left.

53

West Hollywood grew into a complex multi-industry town: a transportation hub, entertainment destination, and as residence to and workshop for employees of the booming movie industry. This photo taken in 1938 portrays the grandeur of the Sunset Strip, with the mansions built above Sunset Towers and the Hacienda Arms gazing down at the scene below. The end of the decade, even with Depression nipping at the studios' heals, did little to dampen the enthusiasm of those investing in West Hollywood and its future. The hillside enclave of movie-makers, stars, grips, carpenters, costumers, and set designers would prosper for decades more.

This view of moviedom was taken from the vicinity of Sunset Towers pointing southwest. In the distance is Twentieth Century Fox's water tower. On the horizon is the Pacific Ocean. A limitless horizon, it seemed to the movie business, where shadow seldom fell and it never rained on your parade. Many of West Hollywood's most famous apartment towers can be seen here, including Harper House, Casa Granada, and the Mirador. The outdoor mall the stars and the apartment dwellers frequented, Sunset Plaza, is pictured beneath.

The Hollywood Golden Age lasted through the Depression, and the studio system survived through World War Two. This formerly desolate little strip of land between a mountain, a set of railroad tracks, and swamp fill called West Hollywood by residents and Hollywood by the world found incredible prosperity.

West Hollywood sat astride both the working studios of Hollywood and the enclaves of movie moguls, actors, and directors of Beverly Hills. The resultant mixed community had low and high-end housing, intense commercial activity, a busy transport hub, was low-tax and low-maintenance, and had almost nonexistent overhead. There was little in the way of law enforcement by the weak and ineffective county government. The formula was set: creativity plus industry plus refugees plus freedom would add up to make the unincorporated enclave one of the most progressive-thinking places in America, and while the area's faces would change again and again with the times, the one thing that would not change would be adherence to that forward-looking and progressive set of ideals.

# *Four*

# STUDIOS AND
# RECORDS RULE

Russell Westcott grew up in Sherman watching his father work inside the Sherman Shops as a cabinetmaker making the interiors seen here. In 1956 he recalled being fascinated as a child by the airbrake section and the testing of the brakes. Westcott received rides around the yard from friends of his father and he eventually became a motorman for the Pacific Electric. He recalled the diggers cutting the Sunset cut at Silver Lake, Benton Way, and Occidental. "The big shovel worked with mules and scrapers, hand laborers, wagons and dirt trucks to Occidental substation where it was sent to the swamp behind Sherman yards for fill." He also recalled the difference between Santa Monica and the Sunset Strip. "Oh, there was a difference, right there was. Up on the hill they were fancy and down here, well, with the tracks and trains and all on the street, it was grimy and noisy."

The original four members of the United Artists studio added additional partners, such as Samuel Goldwyn, Norma Talmadge, Gloria Swanson, and Joseph Schenk. Their productive capacity, due in large part to the many huge sound stages on the lot in West Hollywood, kept them in the forefront of studios through the depression. In 1933 Schenk split off to found 20th Century Productions. Goldwyn emerged as the power broker in the group. These people played a large role in nurturing, and then controlling, the very beginnings of Hollywood from the studio on Formosa and Santa Monica Boulevard. Pictured here, from left to right, beginning at the top row, are Charlie Chaplin, Darryl Zanuck, Samuel Goldwyn, Mary Pickford, Joseph Schenk, and Douglas Fairbanks.

The biggest studio in town, United Artists, stayed big and grew stronger under Sam Goldwyn's strong hand. Alexander Korda had joined Goldwyn at UA in 1937, along with Merle Oberon. By 1939 the sign on the front gate of the read Samuel Goldwyn Studios.

Along that very street, Santa Monica Boulevard, businesses of all types grew strong along with the studio, including massage parlors, steam baths, and many taverns. These blue collar bars gave the railway workers and film laborers a place to blow off steam. The environs might not have matched the luxury of the Players Club or the Mocombo, but were effective nonetheless.

Established in 1920, Barney's Beanery (pictured right, at the end of the auto shops) catered to the auto mechanics, carpenters, and grips who lived in the neighborhood and worked at Goldwyn or 20th Century. Barely discernable in the top photo but behind and above Barney's Beanery is Sunset Towers. Barney's became a major rock hangout in the 1960s, as performers rolled down the hill from the Strip to eat and drink after gigs. The restaurant and bar's policies also became the focus of the new city's gay political power upon incorporation in 1984. United Artists continued to expand, adding new sound stages and facilities on their Santa Monica Boulevard lot. This photo makes one wonder if they hadn't used all the land in Hollywood by then.

So closely did the bucolic and the industrial jostle one another it seemed that the town itself was a sound stage, if the land governed by the county could be called a town. These photos were taken a year apart and less than a quarter mile apart. The first looks over the West Hollywood border into Beverly Hills at Sunset, the second is on the Sherman yards directly below and just east. The class divide between the Santa Monica corridor, the Sunset Strip, and the Hollywood Hills above remains today.

But "cultural" gaps between the coddling offered to the stars (and their pets) on the Strip and rough and tumble activities of the workmen below (not to mention the gambling and strip joints catering to both) only pointed out how much the area had become one in which people with a high tolerance for "difference" or "diversity" in adult entertainments gathered for their own. Even though the town's working class foundation long preceded the influx of the stars on the Strip, the world's gaze turned, when it turned to West Hollywood, to the Strip and the glamour that the stars cast off with such panache.

"West Hollywood developed from a railway yard," said Sheldon Andelson, a civic leader in West Hollywood. "It was considered a kind of Gold Coast environment during the earliest days—with a lot of railway workers and a lot of bars and taverns, even on Sunset." On August 17, 1941, the last trolley went down the boulevard to the ocean. Freight continued to be hauled on the Santa Monica tracks in the night-time hours until 1961.

While the Santa Monica transportation and business corridor labored in anonymity, the Sunset Strip grew into one of the world's most exclusive shopping destinations, and the favorite playground of the new Hollywood royalty. Hotels like the Chateau Marmont, pictured here, gathered stars to them like mice to cheese. Rivaling Beverly Hills for shopping and dining, the stars eagerly shopped the Montgomery Family's development, Sunset Plaza. Through the war soldiers on leave were brought by the busloads to clubs along the Strip, sending its fame far and wide. The Sunset Strip reigned as America's premier entertainment mecca through the 1930s, and well into the 1950s when the studio system began to fray and Las Vegas was developed.

This 1955 photo of Maxime's Cafe captures the feel of life on the Sunset Strip at the time. Wilder's film *Sunset Boulevard* in 1950 spurred even more interest in the Sunset Strip, bringing travelers from around the world to gaze at the hillside strip. The California sun, the warmth, the tolerant attitude for anything new and different, and the many fine dining establishments like Maxime's, all played a role in developing the area as a major tourist destination. The strip would again become a world-class destination for shopping, eating, and night-clubbing, but only after an interregnum caused by the advent of Las Vegas in the Nevada desert.

As tourism increased after World War II so too did hotel space and nightclubs to accommodate the crowds. The stars still held sway over the fabled Sunset Strip, entertaining in the nightclubs and turning out to support their friends. The hillside swath of lights and music was protected by the benign neglect of an overworked county government. In this view we can see many of the

newer hotels and apartments that lined the Strip, and also the high-rises of nearby Hollywood in the rear right. The density of the area has increased, with buildings built higher after earthquake safety precautions took effect in the 1950s and 1960s.

In 1948 the Supreme Court ruled that movie studios could not own the houses in which patrons viewed their films. That ruling shook the studio system to the core. In addition, television threatened, even panicked, the movie industry, which responded with such innovations as the ill-fated "Smell-o-Vision." The McCarthy Era and the blacklisting of the "Hollywood Ten" cast a pall over the hillside idyll's lights and song. Traditionally busy nightclubs on the Strip, like Ciro's and the Troc, suffered competition in the 1950s from two sides: television and Las Vegas. Both clubs folded under the pressure. However, the Troc rose again and again from its own ashes, and Ciro's became the successful Comedy Store.

But a critical mass of creative types—writers and actors and theater people—had been reached and the movies were still big in West Hollywood, as this opening at the Coronet shows in 1953. All the talent that the film industry drew to California, and to West Hollywood in particular, would be redirected in the next decade, but few knew in 1953 that television would be so ubiquitous by the end of the century. Other critical, and far more stable, cultural components such as churches and synagogues, appeared. Temple Beth El was founded in Hollywood at Wilton and Hollywood in 1922 but soon moved to its current location on Crescent Heights in West Hollywood. The Sunset Tower can be seen catching the sun behind the temple. The large Iranian Jewish community adopted it in 2003.

When CBS constructed its then state-of-the-art television-only station on the grounds of former Gilmore Field in 1952 it became the first studio dedicated wholly to production of filmed television. With ABC establishing itself on the east side of Hollywood and NBC just over the hill in Burbank, West Hollywood had a seat at television's table. The jump-start television gave to the youth-oriented service-and-entertainment economy through the 1950s and 1960s, given West Hollywood's low rents and close proximity to acting jobs, cannot be underestimated. West Hollywood became *the* place for aspiring actors from the world over, adding yet another layer of respect for difference. Gays and lesbians began migrating to the relative safety of the weakly-policed county protectorate, becoming a sizeable and visible minority in a community that had always welcomed refugees from oppression.

The 1960s youth culture brought with it a decline in the businesses along the Strip that had catered to the stars. The clubs were now neglected places where young entrepreneurs could eke out a living by buying and operating coffee shops or clubs that played live music. Doug Weston ran the Troubadour where Elton John and Joni Mitchell played often. The club owners in West Hollywood qualified for youth permits from the county that allowed them to admit minors as long as they were not served liquor, giving them a chance to hang out and listen to the newest music. Gazzari's, a rock mainstay on the Strip for over 25 years, says goodbye in this photo taken in 1981. The Troubadour is still open and successful, as is the Whiskey and the Rainbow Room (formerly Largo).

Once the Beatles broke the rock lock in American pop, the Strip became the breeding ground for a multitude of seminal American rock bands to play, including the Doors, Frank Zappa, the Mamas and the Papas, the Byrds, the Velvet Underground, Canned Heat, and more. New offices opened by Phil Spector and Mike Curb on the Strip replaced the agents who ruled there ten years before, and literally picked up and moved the power center of music from New York to Los Angeles. Recording studios sprang up all over West Hollywood and Hollywood with studio musicians working on both film and record projects. The nature of the Strip changed from neatly coiffed stars to youths, many in long hair or motorcycle garb. Youths from all over the country were drawn to the Strip and its environs—and were sometimes homeless, spilling down the hill to find a sofa or sugar daddy.

Increasing land values were driving up housing costs in the 1960s and 1970s, threatening the bohemian characteristics of the enclave. As developers built hotels on the Strip, and houses increased in value, the cost of renting a home or apartment nearby went up. "It was once a place where a young man could come to and live inexpensively and explore himself, or a place where a senior citizen could hope to retire and obtain adult services easily. I'm afraid the youths of today don't have much of a chance to get their start here today, and seniors are having a harder and harder time of it," said Jeff Prang, mayor of West Hollywood in 2003.

SUNSET

SANTA MONI[CA]

MELROSE

As shown here in this aerial view of West Hollywood *c.* 1964, all the formerly vacant land in the area had been filled in with apartments, homes, or businesses. With the town nestled between Hollywood and Beverly Hills, the West Hollywood corridor served nearly everyone in the movie business in some way, shape or form. Notice the blackened area to the left where the

Sherman Yards had been, and, at the time of this photo, demolished and cleared. CBS Studio is just off the picture to the right and the bottom, at Beverly and Fairfax. Fairfax High School is shown just above it on Melrose Avenue.

This photo shows the transit through West Hollywood, formerly Sherman, of the very last train to pass down Santa Monica Boulevard in 1965. While trolley service had ceased in the early 1940s, freight was run during the evening hours until the Johnson Administration. The tracks remained the property of Southern Pacific for decades longer, and were left in a state of disheveled disrepute even after the car barns and shops were torn down to make room for a bus terminal. Above the train and to the west shine the lights of the Sunset Strip.

Meanwhile, above that train, rock and roll bands and groupies flocked to Gene Autry's Hotel Continental, later known as the Hyatt House, the sight of some of the most storied hotel room destructions ever recorded in the tabloids. The parties sometimes lasted days. In this picture Ciro's was still in business, but would not be for much longer as the rock craze took over the Strip.

The Famous *Players Restaurant* — Hollywood, Cal.

In another sign of the changing times, Preston Sturges' club and upscale restaurant Players Club had failed in these more informal times. Not even the Chateau Marmont could keep it going. The restaurant became a succession of failed restaurants until the Imperial Gardens took over in the 1970s to serve Japanese food. Today a restaurant called Miyagi's does business from the location.

Here is shown the Player's Club replacement, the Imperial Gardens, which reigned supreme on the Strip through the record industry days and into the 1980s. In this view the Chateau Marmont looms large above a shadowed Imperial Gardens.

This view up Palm from Santa Monica shows the close but distant relationship between the high rises springing up along the Strip and the transportation corridor below. Both areas were neglected, even forgotten, by county bureaucrats, administrators, and safety personnel such as police and fire. The Strip and the Boulevard both went without needed services. The newly entrenched and vastly rich recording industry that had taken over the Strip didn't much care, but the neglect began to rile some activists and renters in the area enough that they would force studies determining a City of West Hollywood's viability. The study suggested a city would survive quite well, but there wasn't enough interest.

This picture provides a panoramic view into the heart of West Hollywood and its history. Beginning in the lower right quadrant is an oil well, a remnant of the Gilmore Oil Fields rigs that stood in the surrounding land for decades. In 2003, the oil rig is partially hidden between a wall and the Beverly Center along San Vicente Boulevard. On the other side of the street are the beginnings of Cedars-Sinai Hospital, a world-class and world-famous institution built with movie and television money. Up toward the mountains stand towers built with gold records jutting up from the Sunset Strip.

Clutching to the sides of the hills looking down at their adult urban paradise, owners of Richard Nuetra and Frank Lloyd Wright homes such as these declared pointedly to all that design and placement mattered. In fact, interior design and architecture flourished in West Hollywood in the 1950s, due in large part to photographers Theda and Emerson Hall. The couple moved to West Hollywood after World War II and began to buy vacant lots along Melrose Avenue. Following the lead of a few landowners on Beverly Boulevard, the Halls began to draw interior design and furniture makers to the small shops they built on former boysenberry plots. "We decided we wanted to switch Melrose to a street of wholesale showrooms by renting to decorators. We wouldn't rent to anybody else but wholesale showrooms," Theda Hall said in 1985.

Adventurous design and dramatic hillside settings for many buildings made West Hollywood a showroom for 20th century architecture. Here can be seen at the hilltop a Neutra home. Schindler and his gaggle of followers would experiment with the light and warmth of the Southern California climate and create some unique architectural gems, not to mention entire industries once the Schindler-inspired ranch-style pre-fab home was invented. The city's willingness to be avant-garde architecturally, and the Halls' efforts to make Melrose a design corridor, culminated in one of the biggest and most successful architectural stories of the modern age.

Here developers announce their plans for the 750,000 Center Blue building of their proposed Pacific Design Center (PDC). The development, slated to be completed over several decades, would eventually take up most of the land that the Sherman rail yards once inhabited. Catering to the trade only, the building is meant to attract even more interior design business to West Hollywood.

These drawings show the appearance of the completed structure, a cobalt blue monolith with glass sheathing. The building initially had trouble finding sufficient tenants, but did act as a magnet, drawing design firms to the immediate vicinity, accelerating the importance of the West Hollywood design district.

Stage two of the PDC, a building named Center Green, pictured here, was completed in 1988. A skywalk joined the buildings in 1991. Yet another example of the area's urban sophistication, the PDC's international success fueled a further development of the hotel business, the restaurant and entertainment business, and even the music business. John Blandford, a Chicago University-trained economist specializing in gay employment patterns, notes that these highly urbanized and adult-focused industries often employ and draw to them large numbers of gays. "Hotels, design, entertainment, and the food service industry, all these are areas of employment that are highly tolerant of, even seek out, gays," he said. It makes sense, then, that an area focused on hospitality and design would have a higher concentration of gays than other, less design and tourist oriented, places.

This pattern played itself out in West Hollywood, which drew more and more gays, lesbians, transvestites, transsexuals, sexual experimenters, swingers, bisexuals, and polyamours to live and work in the area. Until the mid-1980s the majority of these people lived safely tucked away from distracted and disinterested county bureaucrats in cheap little trolley apartments lining Santa Monica Boulevard.

They lived along Santa Monica Boulevard and did business there, developing a coterie of adult oriented gay shops serving their needs. Many of those began to center below the Strip near this spot at San Vicente and Santa Monica, which became known as "Boystown." The new bus depot is seen here at the top of the shot, and the tracks that the trains used still lie under the dirt and gravel median that separate lanes of traffic.

Gays lived beside seniors and Jews in West Hollywood, and each group respected and tolerated each other. They all had something in common—they all rented. At the time, rents were cheap, and the people respected each other, and things were quietly prosperous. And then, like the high-rise hotels and apartments pictured here, the rents shot up.

*Five*

# DRIVE TO CITYHOOD

Much had happened in the 100 years since the arid wilds of West Hollywood had discouraged surveyors and jackrabbits from putting down roots on its parched hillsides. West Hollywood, by virtue of its location nestled amongst the hills of Hollywood, the stars of Beverly Hills, and the movie, record, and television industries, had become one of the most desirable places in all of Los Angeles to live and work. Older, historic apartment houses like this one were renovated or maintained, while the construction of new high-rise apartment and business rentals went up nearby. Views of the Los Angeles basin greeted thousands each day from their apartment aeries. Businesses increasingly chose the spit of land nestled between Beverly Hills and Los Angeles as the best location for their pursuits.

When television moved to the West Coast, it made West Hollywood an important destination. Quinn Martin Productions used Goldwyn Studios to film its numerous dramas. Nearby CBS Studios made soap operas and dramas, as well as the most popular game show of all, such as *The Price is Right*. This meant work for hundreds of young actors and stagehands, which, along with the traditionally low rents for apartments, made West Hollywood a destination for these predominantly young and single men, many of whom were gay.

The Pacific Design Center acted as an international market draw, bringing buyers from around the world. "The beauty of the Design Center is that it was able to tie together an entire area and make it an international market rather than just a regional one. The entire Pacific Basin is decorated out of this area—I mean the West Coast, Hawaii, Japan, Hong Kong, and Indonesia," said Ron Kates of the West Hollywood Chamber of Commerce.

Meanwhile, Si Frumkin, pictured above at center, and other Jews in West Hollywood began agitating for the release of Russian Jews from behind the Iron Curtain in the 1970s. Frumkin would go on to be an influential voice in Jewish and Zionist circles. His efforts, and efforts of the many Jewish immigrants and refugees who had settled in the area along Fairfax in and near West Hollywood led to large numbers of Russian, and later other Slavic Jews, immigrating to West Hollywood and the surrounding area in the late 1970s through the 1980s and 1990s, especially after the crumbling of the Soviet Union.

One historian said, "The Sunset Strip, both during the Hollywood Golden Age and as the birthplace of the American rock recording industry, exemplifies that American embrace of change and tolerance for new ideas; another example of that embrace of change is the growth in the 1970s and 1980s of the gay strip." Neither the vast numbers of gay men congregating to the television or design work, nor Jewish refugees flocking to the unincorporated space between Beverly Hills and Hollywood alone made West Hollywood a city. It was rent and tenants' issues that catalyzed the movement to become a city. In 1978 85 percent of city rented, 50 percent were Jewish and 30 percent were gay.

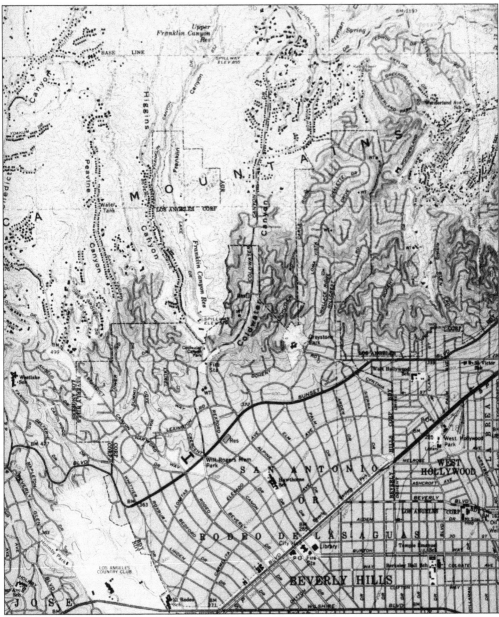

As can be seen here on this map of the area west of La Brea, the unincorporated West Hollywood abuts the super-wealthy Beverly Hills. Increasing land values in Beverly Hills and surrounding areas drove up housing costs in West Hollywood in the 1960s and 1970s, threatening the bohemian characteristics of the enclave. People recognized the dangers in losing that seed-bed. Larry Gross began the Coalition for Economic Survival in response to those issues, a "grassroots multiracial organization representing low- and moderate-income people working to achieve social, economic, and political justice," which operated mainly in South Central and Pico Union, but also among the elderly in West Hollywood. The group used tenant organizing as a tool to "secure the rights of people to have affordable housing, be able to pay utility rates, have transportation, health care, and jobs at decent wages." They would also use tenant organizing to create the newest city in Los Angeles County. CES would be the biggest force behind the incorporation of West Hollywood.

*The Nation* magazine described the situation looming before renters and West Hollywood voters in the 1984 cityhood election: " . . . West Hollywood, like 77 other unincorporated swatches, remained under the loose and often negligent control of the Los Angeles County Board of Supervisors. The absence of civil law produced a kind of civic lawlessness. A stretch of Sunset Boulevard in West Hollywood turned into a jungle of rowdy bars, garish stores and roadside eyesores known as the Sunset Strip: urban development as commercial metastasis. An anemic rent control law sanctioned healthy annual increases, easy evictions, conversions of apartments to hotels and the immediate decontrol of vacant space. Even that lame legislation was due to expire [in 1985], at which point the social and economic character of the community, not to mention the lives of most of its inhabitants, would have drastically and irrevocably changed." Pictured here are the high-rises that created so much resentment in the minds of citizens scrambling to pay their ever-increasing rents. People felt powerless and they felt that landlords, not county government, called the shots. The seeds for cityhood were planted, and the developers watered those seeds assiduously by planning condo and hotel conversions in the many apartment buildings renters relied on for an urban lifestyle.

In the late 1970s the gays were flexing their muscle, taking issue with a sign that hung inside Barney's Beanery that said "Fagots Stay Out." Protests ran daily for weeks at one point, giving gays confidence that they could organize around an issue. By the 1980s, the stresses on tenants forced the seniors (mostly Jewish) and the gays to join forces to protect their interests. The writing was on the wall, and would soon replace Barney's "Fagots Stay Out" sign.

Ron Stone had been an aide to Senator Alan Cranston before focusing on West Hollywood cityhood. Stone, now called the "Father" of West Hollywood, needed a seasoned political grassroots organization to organize the campaign, and CES, which was looking at ways to address renter's issues before the county, saw Stone as a bridge to the gay renter community. The two groups formed a shaky coalition that eventually placed incorporation, a subject long researched and discussed, on the ballot in 1984.

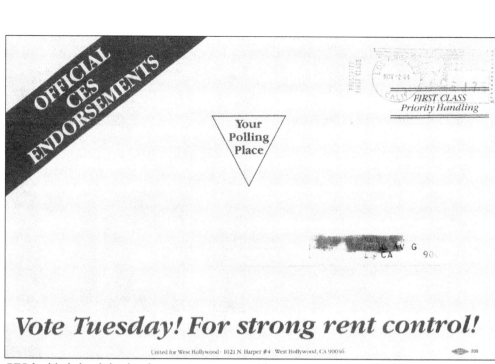

Your Polling Place

FIRST CLASS
Priority Handling

## Vote Tuesday! For strong rent control!

United for West Hollywood · 1021 N. Harper #4  West Hollywood, CA 90046

CES had led the fight for the previous countywide rent control law that was set to expire in 1985 and was responsible for sparking the West Hollywood cityhood campaign. Membership in CES at time was about 8,000, including almost 2,000 in West Hollywood, giving the coalition a diverse and powerful mix of gays and seniors with which to push for incorporation. Gilda Hass, CES member, recalled the campaign, "It really happened. Older Jewish women were working in the campaign office and ringing doorbells alongside young gay men. The thing that united them was that they were convinced they were working for their rights."

**The CES renters' rights team:**

| John Heilman | Doug Routh | Helen Albert |

**CES also endorses:**

| Alan Viterbi | Valerie Terrigno |

Landlords, and the Montgomery Family in particular, opposed the plan to incorporate. Banks Montgomery represented the old-money business and land interests on the Strip. These interests were opposed to cityhood and they created a "push" poll asking voters if they approved of homosexuals "pouring into" their city. As can be seen here on this mailer sent in the days before the vote, Coalition for Economic Survival endorsed four of the five top vote-getters in the first city council elections. The only CES candidate who did not fare well enough to make the council was Doug Routh.

94

Valerie Terrigno, who went on to win the mayor's spot, stressed in the campaign that West Hollywood would not become a "gay city," this despite the fact that 20 of the 40 people running for city council were gay and the Gay Pride parade (pictured here) ran right through West Hollywood. During the cityhood campaign, gays expressed hopes that West Hollywood would emerge as a haven for the oppressed, a place as free as possible of discrimination, both official and subtle. The reality was that a successful move into self-government would make the presence of gays in public life a lot less of a curiosity to the world. "Sexual preference is irrelevant to professional service," said John Heilman, a future city council member.

But the reality was that gays were becoming cognizant of their growing power, manifested each year in the gay pride festivals held in the center of West Hollywood. There was a sense of empowerment in the area, resulting in gays asking, "Why not govern ourselves?" As quoted in *The Nation*: "The frustrations of the refugees [landing in West Hollywood—the last stop for the dispossessed] grew out of the persistent denial of privilege, status, and legitimacy in the face of the opportunities and conveniences of ghetto life. But if fifteen years of gay liberation movement suggested any strategy for legitimization, it was the exercise of political power. Most homosexuals learned long ago that quiescence does not lead to acceptance by the heterosexual world. Even though the gays of West Hollywood do not resemble most militant in other ghettos, they intuit the same lessons of empowerment, organization, and activism."

The union of experienced Jewish activists fighting to free their fellows from discrimination and tyranny in other lands, seniors like those on the float below who were just fed up with rent increases and conversions, and urban gays who simply wanted to have a voice for once, created, by an overwhelming margin, the City of West Hollywood.

Soon after the city's formation, John Stodder, aide to Ed Edelman, then-County Supervisor of the area of West Hollywood, asserted, " . . . two issues face the city after rent control and discrimination ordinances are put into place. Those [first two] are easy and they have a mandate. The endemic problems are development, services, and parking. Investors want to make West Hollywood Beverly Hills Jr., and the elder Jewish renters fear the loss of their urban lifestyle to gentrification and high rents."

The voters determined that they were up to facing those investors and problems and voted a mostly CES slate, including three homosexuals, into city council. Alan Viterbi, Steve Schulte, Valerie Terrigno, John Heilman, and Helen Albert pose for the ceremonial picture above. The new City Council's first actions, taken on the night of incorporation ceremonies and taking three minutes to introduce and pass unanimously, were banning discrimination of all kinds against gays, seniors, women, religions, and races; approving a moratorium on new development; a rent rollback and ban on evictions pending adoption of a rent control ordinance, which was introduced in late spring 1985. When the city council approved the first job non-discrimination ordinance based on sexual orientation, the new mayor, Terrigno, saw people crying in the audience. "I realized that we never had a place that was safe," she said. "We could still be fired from our job for being gay just a few blocks away." That same council meeting brought the banning of the requirement for more than one ID from blacks, asians, and hispanics upon entering clubs—this striking down a discriminatory practice by bar owners that the county had allowed to fester.

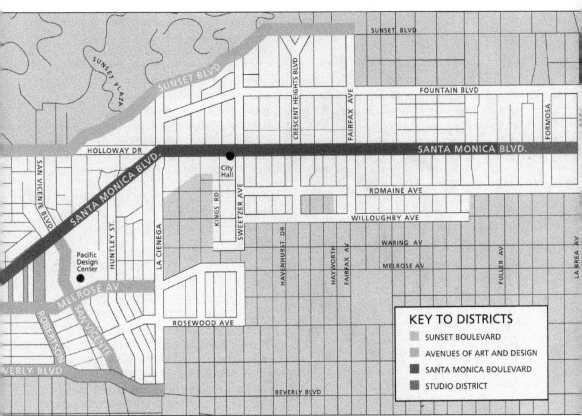

City Attorney Michael Jenkins described the first heady days of legislating liberty and non-discrimination. "There is nothing more challenging than setting precedents and drawing up new laws that have never been tried before. When you finally add them all together you will find very few if any cities that have done all the things we have done." Los Angeles County Local Agency Formation Commission estimated before the election that West Hollywood's tax revenues (a one percent sales tax) would be nearly $15 million, with expenses just shy of $10 million, leaving quite a surplus. The city would find even greater surpluses, $7.5 million, in the first year. The surpluses the city's coffers rang up in years after cityhood would be used predominantly for infrastructural improvement and for social programs. West Hollywood spends huge amounts of money on senior care and housing, nutrition, HIV/AIDS, family activities, sporting activities, etc. It turned out that the "Gay Camelot" had quite a treasury at its disposal.

The concerns of CES, and those of seniors renters and gays, were given top priority by the seniors, gays, and renters on the council, like those pictured at left. Under their leadership West Hollywood became first city in 1985 to declare Yom Kippur a holiday, giving city employees the day off and shutting down in honor of the Jewish holiday. The progressive social legislation continued. By April 1985 the council passed an ordinance prohibiting the city from investing its funds in banks or institutions that do business in or with South Africa. The council also unanimously supported the Grape Boycott in 1985. "To what degree have we been elected to be innovative? This isn't just a 'gay' city. We have a real chance to create a model city, showing groups in other areas how they can bring about change on issues such as access to their officials and recognition of equal pay for equal work," said Mayor Terrigno. A local gay newsmagazine applauded the new city with this: "These pioneering resolutions [West Hollywood's spate of anti-discrimination ordinances] defined values that all five council members share, and they are honorable concepts of which we can all be proud. It is sad that such values are not universal beyond the city's borders . . . "

It only took six weeks after cityhood before Barney's Beanery was in hot water over its matchbooks, which, like the original sign hanging above their bar, and pictured here being presented to USC's One Institute and Archives in 2003, said "Fagots Stay Out." Ironically, in the early 1960s Barneys had become a gay hangout until the Alcohol Board of Control pressured the original owner, Barney Anthony, to keep gays out.

"That's when the sign went up," Morris Kight said about the ABC's pressure on Anthony. Kight, a self-described "gay activist" and founder of the Gay Liberation Front, had organized the earlier-mentioned protests that spanned weeks, picketing the eatery and conducting "shop ins," in which people would sit at tables for hours with cold coffee. The sign did not come down, however, until January 14, 1985, after the new city passed a misdemeanor ordinance banning discrimination based on sexual orientation. The sign was personally removed by Mayor Terrigno, and then given to Kight, who held it until his death in 2003, when it went to the One Institute and Archives.

The new lesbian mayor, Terrigno, was interviewed countless times by newspapers and televisions stations from around the world due to her sexual orientation and new position of power. She stressed during her campaign that West Hollywood would not become a "gay city." She changed her tune in those interviews, asserting that those who predicted a "Gay Camelot" in West Hollywood might have been right. But while the men partied in Boystown, some claimed the FBI plotted an end to Camelot.

Two signal events occurred on February 7th and 8th, just weeks after incorporation. First, word leaked to the *Los Angeles Times* that Mayor Terrigno was being investigated for embezzlement by the FBI. The following day the city council offered a form of domestic partnership rights to the city's senior and gays. Terrigno was eventually indicted and resigned the largely ceremonial post of mayor in August, 1985. John Heilman, who took over as mayor, said, "We're going to continue to function . . . and we'll continue to work together to solve the problems of the city." Terrignos supporters were adamant that she was framed. "I certainly think (the indictment was filed) because she was the first lesbian mayor," said a supporter, Sallie Fisk, co-chair of the Stonewall Democratic Club. Terrigno was found guilty on all counts of fraud and embezzlement, receiving a jail sentence of 60 days, 1,000 hours community service, and restitution amounting to $8,000. She served on the council until 1995. In 2002, Gov. Gray Davis signed a state-wide domestic partners act designed along the same lines as that municipal domestic partner ordinance passed in 1985.

# *Six*

# THE CREATIVE CITY

Nearly one hundred years earlier, in 1886, H.H. Wilcox arrived in California with his new wife Daeida and bought 120 acres at Cahuenga and Hollywood Boulevard, subdividing it for development as an agricultural-based, Christian temperance enclave. Next door, the area on the left on this map depicted as wilderness and now called West Hollywood, would remain unincorporated and nearly forgotten by historians until it became the newest city in Los Angeles County, the City of West Hollywood, in 1984. At the time of its cityhood it boasted more than a few bars and nightclubs, an urban adult environment, a population over 50 percent Jewish, roughly one third gay, 85 percent renter, and at least 40 percent senior citizen.

# CITY OF WEST HOLLYWOOD

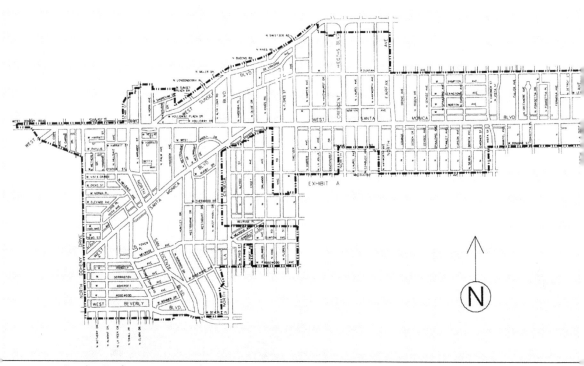

In the *Daily News* on February 24, 1985, Sheldon Andelson, a West Hollywood attorney, banker and political power broker, was quoted as saying, "The new city of West Hollywood often is compared to the Bohemian section of Paris along the river Seine. It's sort of a Left Bank to the Beverly Hills-Wilshire Corridor. It's always been something of a sophisticated adult neighborhood. Grown ups live and play here." Issues facing the new council included, obviously, rent control and homosexual and ethnic population issues, but also prostitution, a remnant from the days of lax law enforcement, and developing an infrastructure suitable for doing business with the world entertainment and design community. The ugly unused gash of railroad tracks that split the main street, Santa Monica Boulevard, became an urgent issue. The Southern Pacific had traditionally refused to give up its right to the property to any but the California transportation agency, Caltrans, who had their plans for widening and "beautifying" their State Route 2, the former Route 66 of legend.

The city covered over the tracks running down Santa Monica Boulevard with a grass median and used every means at its disposal to beautify the main strip running through town. West Hollywood resident artists like Keith Haring were invited to install "Urban Art" along the median, resulting in automobile sculpture, Haring's post-modernist human forms, and this display of unique "Lawn Furniture." However, attempts by the city to gain needed improvements and maintenance on the roadbed and along sidewalks from Caltrans were ignored, forcing the city to investigate other ways to address the issues concerning the street.

Russian immigration to West Hollywood sped up through the 1980s as the Soviet Union slowly crumbled. Thousands of 'refuseniks,' who had been trying for years to emigrate to America, were allowed to do so in the days of Glasnost under Soviet leader Mikhael Gorbachev. As the incursion by Russian Jews continued, it became more difficult for long-time residents of West Hollywood to earn livings in the businesses they had built in the unincorporated town. Shatsky and Shapiro, a neighborhood dime store for 16 years, closed in 1985 due to rent increases along Santa Monica Boulevard. Its closing foreshadowed a trend of gentrification that would be common through the 1990s and into the new century. Their supporters criticized "Yuppification" and "Croissantification" for the rise in rents. The landlord, Crocker Real Estate manager of trust J.C. Ogilvie said, "Some of the businesses that have been there are being outbid for their own stores due to the neighborhood's changing."

The numbers of Russian immigrants increased during 1980s and 1990s, making the east end of West Hollywood decidedly Slavic and Jewish. Cultural celebrations were added to existing ones, even though there was some friction that developed between the older, Russian Jews and the younger, gay population. Openly-gay council member Steve Schulte, though, saw the benefits of those new experiences in civic government for the Russians. "They come here from Russia, where gays can be jailed, to West Hollywood, where gays are part of the power structure. It's a tremendous experience for them." The street festival pictured here attests to the new city's diversity: Jews, gays, blacks, and seniors all came together as a community to celebrate their urban lifestyle.

**NONE OF THESE WILL GIVE YOU AIDS**

Eating Utensils     Casual Contact     Using Public Facilities     Social (Dry) Kissing

MYTH: "I can get AIDS if I touch someone who has it, use the same laundry facilities, the same swimming pool, eat in the same restaurant, or if they cough or sneeze on me."

FACT: The chances of getting AIDS from casual non-sexual contact are virtually nil. AIDS is caused by a virus that is *ONLY* transmitted through blood products and intimate sexual contact involving bodily fluids. Even health care workers caring for AIDS patients have not come down with AIDS as a result of their work.

MYTH: "I can get AIDS by using public restrooms."

FACT: You *CANNOT* get AIDS by sitting on a toilet seat. To protect yourself and others from common germs, always wash your hands after using the restroom.

MYTH: "I'm visiting my brother who has AIDS. If I eat with him or sleep on his bed linens I might get AIDS."

FACT: You *CAN* eat with persons who have AIDS, even if they have prepared the food, without fear of contracting AIDS. But, of course, you should always follow safe health practices -- wash your hands before preparing meals, wash dishes in hot, soapy water, and wash clothes and soiled linens in hot water with household bleach -- to protect yourself against *ANY VIRUS*, AIDS included.

MYTH: "Since I'm not gay and don't use intravenous drugs, I'll never get AIDS."

FACT: AIDS is caused by a virus, and anyone who is exposed to it through blood or sexual contact can become infected. You can reduce the risk of getting AIDS by following safe sex guidelines.

MYTH: "If I'm going to have surgery, there is a good chance I could get AIDS from a blood transfusion."

FACT: Recently, a blood screening test was introduced that identifies blood infected by the AIDS virus so that it can be removed from the blood supply. This new test provides us all with a safer blood supply.

**AIDS HOTLINE 213-871-AIDS**

Monday - Friday, Noon - 10 p.m.
Weekdays 10 a.m. - 3 p.m.

**W.H.A.A.M.**

**WEST HOLLYWOOD AIDS AWARENESS MESSAGE**

While the city council turned their attention to running a city, and while Jewish émigrés from a newly opened Soviet Union poured into West Hollywood, the newly discovered disease now called AIDS turned into an epidemic among the city's gay male population. It was just two months after Terrigno's sentencing, in early October 1985, that Rock Hudson died of AIDS. Elizabeth Taylor said of his death, "Pray God it wasn't in vain." Days later the city announced plans to hire the nation's first AIDS lobbyist to negotiate for funding to address the "gay plague" with state legislators. Additionally, the city became the first municipality in the country to design and implement "education" programs about the disease, which in its earliest days was shrouded in mystery, stigma, and fear. Along with New York City and San Francisco, West Hollywood was rapidly becoming an epicenter for the new disease, which seemed to strike mainly gay males. This informational poster called W.H.A.A.M. (West Hollywood AIDS Awareness Message), one of the first such efforts in the nation, attempted to dispel rumors about transmission of the AIDS virus while educating people on symptoms, prevention, and transmission. It was aimed at the 10,000 high-risk gay men living in the city. This poster was initially controversial, but it became a template for numerous other municipalities' efforts to control the spread of AIDS.

The AIDS epidemic further radicalized the lesbian and gay population, becoming the focus for Gay Pride parades and festivals for the next decade. Pride crowds continued to expand, offering men and women at least one day a year they could "come out" and enjoy a day in the sun. Parents and Friends of Lesbians and Gays formed, creating one of many straight ally organizations seeking to nurture freedom and equality for their children, siblings, and friends. They are pictured here parading in 1986 at San Vicente and Santa Monica Boulevard.

West Hollywood, galvanized by the deaths of scores of young gay men, sought ways to fund research and treatment for the community. They joined with local AIDS service agencies that had been formed to provide emotional support and hospice services for AIDS patients to sponsor AIDS Walk in 1985. Large sums of money were given by the city to a variety of organizations to provide surcease from suffering of their citizens who contracted AIDS.

People living in the city's historic residences began complaining that many of them were crumbling, so the city formed a commission in 1987 to survey the city's architectural legacy. After the survey 117 structures were considered to be worth "registering" or preserving, all of them built before 1939. The list included such icons as the Strip's Chateau Marmont, pictured below in 2003 behind Miyagi's Restaurant, which inhabits the original space occupied by Preston Sturges's Players Club. Other significant structures on the list included Schindler House and Patio Del Moro.

The Sunset Tower building sat derelict for several years after several attempts to demolish the building in the late 1970s and early 1980s. In 1986 it was purchased and renovated by the St. James Club of Great Britain. The 14-story landmark stands as an exquisite example of Art Deco architecture and is considered by some to be as much a symbol of Hollywood as the 'Hollywood' sign. At the anniversary ceremony, at which the recent grand opening of the St. James Club was mentioned, Mayor Alan Viterbi, said, "Without a doubt the St. James Club is the city's most important historic landmark." Designed in 1929 by architect Leland A Bryant, the Sunset Tower was a landmark from the moment it opened.

Developer Severyn Ashkenazy, a financier who helped build six hotels in the area, opposed cityhood. He invested, along with other landlords, $2 million in the fight opposing the referendum. His efforts in 1988 to convert apartments to condos and hotel rooms was opposed by a renter-backed city council determined to get adequate protections for tenants and people living near the new hotels. The situation was settled later that year by a $5 million payout over 20 years to the city for back taxes as price for conversion, plus supplying parking and other improvements to the properties. The conversions went ahead after the settlement.

In 1989 gay men reported harassment in the city's parks by sheriff's deputies. Steve Schulte said the incident, "violated an unwritten policy" established after West Hollywood became a city that plainclothes deputies would not make lewd conduct arrests. Capt. Rachel Burgess, the new commander, defended the use of plainclothes officers in making arrests in parks. However, in February the department announced that a recruitment drive focusing on hiring gay sheriff deputies was being considered by then-Sheriff Sherman Block.

Discrimination issues seemed to grow in intensity and importance for the young city. In 1992 a bill brought by West Hollywood assembly member Terry Friedman that would prohibit discrimination against gays in housing and employment in the state of California passed both houses. Then-Governor Pete Wilson had promised city officials and gay activists that he would sign the bill, but he reneged on the promise. In response, Rob Roberts, a West Hollywood resident and Queer Nation activist, wrote in an open letter to the community on September 23, 1991, about the betrayal over Assembly Bill 101 (AB 101) "This is a passionate cry for freedom. I will not eat solid food until you sign AB 101." His private protest swelled to two weeks of public protests centered on his tent in the crescent of land at Santa Monica and Crescent Heights. "I know what discrimination can do in the workplace. I know it can destroy promising careers. This cannot go on," he said.

114

On Tuesday, October 1, 1992, thousands gathered in West Hollywood, burned Wilson in effigy, blew whistles, gave speeches, and marched into Los Angles along Wilshire and Hollywood Boulevards. At one point the protesters surrounded the Los Angeles County Museum of Art where Wilson was meeting the president of Mexico, Arturo Salinas de Gotari. The city gave employees the day off so they could join with protesters from around the state to rally in Sacramento in mid-October. Even though the protests did not result in Wilson's signing the bill, a virtually identical bill was passed and signed into law in 2000. A memorial to Rob Roberts and the protests stands today on the very ground Roberts pitched his tent on and used as his headquarters.

Through the 1990s the Jewish population expanded and grew. The nationality of émigrés was mixed, with Jews from the Eastern Europe and Baltic countries beginning to escape the former-Soviet bloc after the fall of the Berlin Wall. West Hollywood Jews supported Jews in Israel, protested anti-Semitism in Europe and Russia, and agitated for protections for their families and friends back home. A powerful Jewish lobby centered in West Hollywood continued to have an affect on the plight of the Jews in less enlightened countries, even as the city officials sought to keep the large non-English speaking segment of the community safe.

The Sunset Strip thrived in the 1990s, with the clubs and hotels and restaurants again booming. Developers floated new projects, the number of hotel rooms skyrocketed, and international attention to the West Coast's premier entertainment capital increased. The city's coffers filled and the social problems began to fade. Still, anti-smoking agitation succeeded in knocking the world-famous Marlboro Man off his long-time perch atop the gateway to the Strip in the early 1990s. "In the early days we were idealists. Council members were motivated by what was best for the city," commented John Heilman, who still in 2003 holds the council seat he has held since the city's founding, in 1998. "The last five years it's much more political— all about jockeying for political advantage. It's disheartening to lose that idealism."

In the mid-1990s the city bought an office building on the corner of Sweetzer and Santa Monica Boulevard and renovated the structure into a three-floor City Hall. To many, the brand-spanking new modern municipal power-center bespeaks the city government's maturation from a gaggle of inexperienced activists to a seasoned bureaucracy ready to take on the city's problems. Renter's issues declined in importance. The city needed to create funding flows to restore and maintain infrastructure. In 1996, the Steve Martin-led council fired Mark Johnson, a strong renters advocate and the popular director of the city's Rent Stabilization Department. CES was not the force it once was, and the activist agenda has been marginalized in West Hollywood since John Heilman had lost his CES-based majority to Martin in 1994. In a situation some consider indicative of the gentrification of West Hollywood, in 1998 the city purchased land on Kings Road to build affordable housing. When owners of adjacent condos caught wind of the project, they organized to kill it. The faction on the city council that followed Martin helped change the housing into a pocket park. Heilman believed he witnessed a sea change in the city's politics. "It was the first time we defeated affordable housing," Heilman said. "It was disturbing." But Martin contended that Kings Road was a watershed for neighborhood self-determination. He felt that the issues important to CES were no longer issues important to West Hollywood. "CES used to be a political machine, but they managed to somehow blow it," Martin said. "They were good with rent control and social services, not particularly good at listening to what people wanted."

"Gentrification inevitably follows improvements in infrastructure," council member Jeff Prang said in the days following completion of the Santa Monica Boulevard Reconstruction Project. "But we absolutely had to fix the road. There was no other solution." This shot shows the street in front of what had been, in 1919, Jesse D. Hampton Studio and was at the time Warner Brothers Studio. The road in front had been repaved in the 1960s, but left un-maintained until the city was able to negotiate a reconstruction of the road in 1997.

The road that acted as West Hollywood's main street was pitted, bumpy, ill-maintained, and generally a hazard for the cars and trucks using it as the best way between Hollywood and Beverly Hills or Century City. The city tried repeatedly over the years to get Caltrans to maintain it adequately, but failed to get appropriate responses. Finally, in 1997, the city and the state governments agreed to a plan that would give ownership of the road to the city so that it could proceed with repairs and improvements.

The plan, brokered in a series of meetings between city agencies and the public between 1997 and 1998, was to completely rebuild the roadbed, make improvements to the sidewalks, widening them in many areas, and improve the landscaping. A total price tag was set at $15 million, of which $12.3 million was set for the construction of the road and sidewalks. The actual price tag ballooned to $34 million before the project's completion. The task would sorely try the residents, businesses, and city government's patience with one another for the two years it took to complete. Many small "mom-and-pop" businesses could not handle the strain, and went out of business.

The reconstruction project began in 1999. The city promised that it would take only two years and create only a modicum of financial distress. Amidst great hoopla the center strip in West Hollywood ground to a halt while trucks, workers, cranes, and cement jostled to complete the task. Traffic flow on the boulevard, which had always been something of an ordeal for motorists, became a nightmare, particularly during rush hours. Along the street huge sections of sidewalk were ripped out, with new, freshly poured ones in some areas adjacent to old ones; open dirt trenches, street barricades, warning signs, and orange tape were everywhere; and nearly all of the residential side streets were blanketed with automobiles. Not that parking has ever been trouble-free in West Hollywood, especially on the weekends when the party crowd hits the streets. But construction severely exacerbated the situation. "That is our fault," mused the ever-frank council member Sal Guarriello. "We should have built more than one parking garage for the public."

For the most part the project came in on time and on budget and was completed with a minimum of economic loss to the city. According to the city's finance department, there were no significant decreases in the overall amount of sales tax generated from Santa Monica Boulevard businesses due to the project, although businesses experienced episodic slowdowns during the major roadway construction. In anticipation of the beautified Santa Monica Boulevard, many new businesses, such as Aaron Bros. and Whole Foods Market established themselves on Santa Monica Boulevard during the reconstruction.

The newly beautified city went about its business being creative until early September, 2002, when the real world intruded. On September 1, 2002, resident Trev Broudy was savagely beaten by three men from outside West Hollywood in a gay bashing that brought hundreds of angry residents onto the streets in protest. The episode raised awareness in this city of refugees that they were never completely safe. The sheriff's department earned plaudits for its handling of the crisis; the men responsible were arrested and tried. Broudy, however, had not completely recovered from his injuries by 2003.

As the city matured, it appeared to civic leaders that " . . . people don't seem to have the alienation they did four years ago," Council member Steve Martin said in 1998 of a city founded by gay activists, seniors, and rent-control advocates in 1984. "The city has grown up. People are more concerned with quality of life." Indeed, it seemed that the city focused evermore on creating wealth than on social justice issues. Once the Southern California's most radical enclave where Jews, gays, leftists, and seniors rallied around rent-control and social-justice issues, by 1998 West Hollywood had built a stylish new city hall and was preparing for a $17 million face-lift of Santa Monica Boulevard. West Hollywood, some feared, had entered middle age and left its progressive politics behind.

The gentrification of West Hollywood has not seemed to dull the radical edge of some of its residents. After the Federal government's Drug Enforcement Agency raided and closed down the West Hollywood branch of the Los Angeles Cannabis Resources Center, known as "the best-run medical marijuana club in the country," Scott Imler, executive director of the club, and five associates went on an open-ended hunger strike in protest. With the city's approval and assistance, the Cannabis Club set up the months-long protest at the corner of Santa Monica Boulevard and Gardner you see here. The city of West Hollywood also authorized a loan of $350,000 in redevelopment funds to the center, which would not be repaid in the event of forfeiture of the club's assets to the government. It didn't take much to turn out these Russian Jews. Pictured below in 2001 at the beginning of Israel's Intifada. The large Russian and Jewish population of West Hollywood parallels between the creation of the State of Israel and the City of West Hollywood.

The tolerant city that West Hollywood has become is one in which Jewish, Russian, gay, and senior citizen populations reside side-by-side in relative ease and without the oppression and discrimination many of them remember experiencing elsewhere. The city was built on the socially progressive ideals of the Committee for Economic Survival, a grassroots, multiracial organization representing low- and moderate-income people working to achieve social, economic, and political justice. The city worked to advance and secure the rights of people to have affordable housing, to be able to pay utility rates, to have decent and readily available transportation, to have adequate health care, and to have decent jobs at decent wages. Close examination of these principles show how closely connected those ideals hew to Christianity and Judaism in their intent to salve the suffering of the world's oppressed and dispossessed.

The place that started so desolate a jackrabbit might consider better digs, the way station that once acted as a thoroughfare for trains and actor's careers, stands at the dawn of the 21st century as one of the most forward-looking and progressive cities on earth. The Sunset Strip now draws tens of thousands of visitors a year, as does the Santa Monica Boulevard "Gay Strip," pumping millions of dollars a year into the economy. The populace is financially secure, with a median income equal to the state's median income, and an average income exceeding it. The business mix is one that many municipalities envy, with its focus on retailing and design.

While these young girls celebrating Hanukkah in Plummer Park look forward to a secure future of freedom and tolerance in their new land of West Hollywood, the business buzz of the Sunset Strip and the Santa Monica Corridor hums around them. One hundred years of civic activity came to a focus in the city's 20th anniversary. Celebration for a city constantly renewed and re-invented by its populace and by the immigration of gays and straights, of Russians and Czechs, of Jews and Christians. Twenty years of cityhood, one hundred years of tolerance and diversity and hundreds of years of struggle for peace, all come together in 2004 in the City of West Hollywood.

# WEST HOLLYWOOD

## CITY COUNCILMEMBERS

Valerie Terrigno
*November 1984–1995*

Alan Viterbi
*November 1984–April 1988*

Helen Albert
*November 1984–April 1990*

Steve Schulte
*November 1984–April 1990*

John Heilman
*November 1984–Present*

Abbe Land
*November 1986–Mar*

Paul Koretz
*April 1988–March 2001*

Babette Lang
*April 1990–April 1994*

Sal Guarriello
*April 1990–Present*

Steve Martin
*April 1994–Present*

Jeffrey Prang
*March 1997–Present*

John Duran
*March 2001–Pres*

Charged with the responsibility to guide the city along its path, the intrepid members of the West Hollywood city council deserve special mention. None of them were full-time politicians, nor were any paid full-time wages for their service to the community. Since this portrait was pasted together in 2002 Abbe Land has rejoined the council. From top left to right, the council members names and dates of service, are Valerie Terrigno, November 1984–1995; Alan Viterbi, November 1984–April 1988; Helen Albert, November 1984–April 1990; Steve Schulte, November 1984–April 1990; John Heilman, November 1984–present; Abbe Land, November 1986–March 1997, and March 2003–present; Paul Koretz, April 1988–April 2001 (currently a state assemblyman); Babette Lang, April 1990–1994; Sal Guarriello, April 1990-present; Steve Martin, April 1984–2002, Jeffrey Prang, March 1997–present; and John Duran, March 2001–present. Thank you, all of you, for your service to the Creative City–West Hollywood.

Visit us at
arcadiapublishing.com

CPSIA information can be obtained
at www.ICGtesting.com
Printed in the USA
BVHW062306140921
616745BV00006B/902